Fifty Two Sonnets
of
Glory and Grace

Fifty Two Sonnets

of

Glory and Grace

by

Tom Chapman

First published September 2015 by Thomas G Chapman
10 Hilton Street Tamworth NSW Australia

Cover Photograph: Piallamore, near Tamworth, NSW
Photographer: Andrew Pearson

National Library of Australia Cataloguing-in-Publication entry

Creator: Chapman, Tom, 1935- author.

**Title: Fifty Two Sonnets of Glory and Grace / Tom Chapman;
Illustrated by Richard Lewis, Heather Paterson**

ISBN: 9780980748352

**Subjects: Bible--History of Biblical events--Poetry.
Religious poetry, Australian.**

**Other Creators/Contributors:
Lewis, Richard P. 1945 - illustrator.
Paterson, Heather L. 1987 - illustrator.**

Dewey Number: 220

Set in Piranesi It BT

Foreword

Though Tom and I have never met, we feel like we know each other, and certainly enjoy a warm friendship together. Tom is an Aussie and I am a Yankee living in Chile, but we still have much in common besides our names. We both are sinners saved by the grace of God; we both enjoy a godly heritage, though Tom's goes back much farther than mine; and each of us has a love for music and local church ministry and has been heavily involved in both these avenues of service the greater part of our lives.

How did we connect? Well, Tom saw my name on Sermon Audio and listened to a sermon I preached while in the U.S. on furlough, did an internet search and found our mission website, and through the mission found us!

As I pondered over the sonnets, I began to realize that in these beautiful rhyming expressions, I was reading a sort of mini-commentary in poetic form on a variety of biblical themes, themes that deal with all sorts of practical issues in life, but solidly built on unchanging doctrinal truths. They deal with the reality of life on this planet. Tom looks at sin and its consequences - turmoil, judgement and eternal suffering, but also God's gracious offering of forgiveness and its consequences— peace, acceptance and eternal glory. He considers the universality of human suffering, whether saint or sinner, and the ultimate suffering— death, and how different is its perspective for the unbeliever than that of the believer: terrifying for the one and peaceful, even desirable, for the other. Godliness is extolled and the cruelty of sin condemned. We see

God's immutability and sovereignty, but also his grace and mercy. These sonnets will touch your emotions as they have mine. The truth is, they have moved me from sadness to grief, to anger, to peace, to hope, to joy, to longing for heaven.

Here are a few examples to whet your appetite:
The brevity of life
    How quickly is the span of life consumed,
    How soon, it seems, the years of life are spent.
The incertitude of life
    I saw the reaper pass close by one year,
    And thought he would confront me face to face
    And there and then remove me from my place.
The vanity of life without God
    Their few brief years on earth shall soon pass by,
    Then all the comforts they have ever known
    Shall vanish as they reap what they have sown.
            or
    In vain so many fight the cracking crust
    Of this decaying product of the dust.
Suffering in this life is inevitable
    We shan't traverse this life without a tear
    While waiting for our Saviour to appear.

God's omniscience

But God, the Lord of all creation, knows
Not only deeds and words, but thoughts as well.

God's wrath and mercy

God's wrath is great; His mercy more than great
For all who come to Christ, their advocate.

The reason we should rejoice

What if the day be difficult and long?
What if the spirit flags beneath the load?...
Rejoice! It's Jesus Christ who sits supreme
Above the storms and tragedies and strife.

Our hope

No matter where the yesterdays I trod,
I have become the righteousness of God.

The blessing of a godly life

She smiled and held the new-born to her breast,
She smiled, as through the years she had been blest.
She smiled again, a grateful, tired soul,
And thanked the Lord; but time had taken toll.
She smiled in death, for she had seen her Lord.

Jesus

But how did Jesus Christ become a man?
Both fully God and fully man in one?

————

And yet His Son has felt the pangs of hell
To clothe with righteousness the ones He chose.

———

When Jesus Christ, who is their life, appears
   They'll have a glory past the reach of years.

———

But Jesus says to mankind so distressed,
"Come all to me and I will give you rest."

Above all else, we see Jesus. Jesus is the central figure throughout the sonnets, that which ties all of them together to form one cohesive whole. He is the jewel whose radiance dims all the others. If he is not mentioned by name, his activity "behind the scenes" is implicit. I would say that the central theme of all Tom's sonnets is the grace of God offered through Jesus Christ for the redemption, salvation, and hope of eternal life for all who will trust in him. This gospel message is what gives hope to all of us sinners, and I believe is the driving force behind all of these wonderful poems.

If you are a believer, these verses will convict you of indifference and wasted opportunities, but will also comfort you in your afflictions and increase your desire to live on a higher spiritual plane, making the days yet remaining to you count more for eternity. If you are searching for the truth, you will find many practical biblical answers here, but above all, that Jesus is the only answer you really need. All that is good and satisfying in this life — and the next — flows from him.

A final word: One reading of the sonnets will not do. They are not Scripture, but are full of scriptural tenets. And in a similar manner that a biblical text will yield new insights with each reading, so each time you return to these sonnets, you will find more here to bless your soul than you did the time before. That certainly has been my experience!

I am deeply grateful to Tom for granting me the honor of penning this foreword. It is my prayer that your life will be as enriched as mine has been by the careful and repeated readings of these words from the pen of a true saint of God.

Tom Chapman
Antofagasta, Chile
July 2015

Contents

Acknowledgements

Although the writing and compiling of an anthology is a labour of love, it still requires constant attention, and so I am grateful to those who have been kind and diligent enough to carefully proof read this text for both spelling and grammar content, as well as for doctrinal content and structure.

Firstly then I am indebted to my wife, Gwenda, who, being a crossword fanatic, has a mind for spelling and grammar.

I have appreciated and benefitted, over many years, from the teaching of diligent pastors who have faithfully expounded God's word and had an important part in my spiritual journey, which finds me where I am today. Without such teaching it would not have been possible to compile this collection of sonnets. But, more immediately, has been the valuable discussions with two of the present pastors, Ross Fotheringham and Warwick Lyne. I thank them immensly.

Also there is another Tom Chapman, a missionary friend of mine in Chile, who agreed to read through this collection and provide a foreword, therefore introducing this book to the readers. His finding time for this task is very much appreciated.

I have appreciated the discussions with a fellow poet, Michael Thorely, who checked through these sonnets to verify their integrity from a poetic point of view. As a result some revision of punctuation and wording has been made.

The front cover image was selected from a vast number of impressive landscape photographs of Tamworth professional photographer, Andrew Pearson, who has the knack of capturing the beauty of God's creation. More of his work may be seen at:

www.andrewpearsonphotography.com.au

Perhaps one of the most difficult parts of this work has been providing conceptual illustrations of, at times, very abstract ideas. Richard Lewis and Heather Paterson willingly accepted the project, but I wondered whether sometimes it felt that it was almost an impossible task. However they have successfully completed the challenge. (See Appendix 2)

Of course the most important thanks goes to Jesus Christ, through whom all these truths have been made known and available to mankind, as well as giving everyone involved in this project the abilities to do what they have done. Each one of us is fearfully and wonderfully made by the One who holds the hearts of kings in His hand, and upholds the universe by the word of His mouth, and through Him alone salvation is provided from the just wages of sin for all who come to Him in humble confession of their eternal need.

Tom Chapman,
Tamworth, Australia,
September 2015.

Introduction

They are small, but not so small that they cannot contain seeds of usefulness. They are large enough to present an idea, but not so large that they cannot be easily digested mentally in one sitting. They are sonnets—fourteen lines of medium length with enough room to say something, but short enough to see from one end to the other. Although the sonnet is an old classical form, it still has a great appeal to the present writer, who, though being of considerable age, is, by some hundreds of years, younger than the classical sonnet.

The English essayist, Francis Bacon (1561–1626), wrote: "Read not to contradict and confute; nor to believe and take for granted; nor to find talk and discourse; but to weigh and consider."

You, dear reader, may or may not agree with what you read in these pages, but I urge you to consider what is presented. These thoughts are as I see things, but it is not only from a human standpoint, but also from the perspective of one who takes the Bible as the presented truth of sovereign God.

Should you take exception to what you find here, I invite you to check it against God's revealed word to man, The Bible. Should you take exception to that, the only recourse is to take it up with God Himself.

If you agree with the thoughts presented here, still check against the Bible, for in doing so you will perhaps not only become more familiar with it, but also better equip yourself for life and eternity.

Tom Chapman
Tamworth NSW
Australia 2015.

Sonnets

1

Harvest Time

I saw the Reaper pass close by one year,
And thought He would confront me face to face
And there and then remove me from my place.
The day was dank, the mood was dark and drear.
And yet His sudden visit held no dread
For one who knows of life's incertitude,
And can accept the Reaper might intrude
Without a word of warning being said.
Some fruits are taken early, others late;
And who can tell the ripeness of their crop?
The Reaper's scythe and sickle none can stop;
Already He has set each harvest date.
My harvest time is yet unknown to me,
But God's peace gives assured security.

2

The Psalms

Late evening, when the candle flickers low
And all is silent; nothing to distract
The train of thought, in rushing cataract,
Or meandering in its quiet gentle flow,
The soul might sense some lofty heights of praise
And look toward the things of heaven above;
Or else perhaps, with pain of earthly love,
Might contemplate some coming darker days,
Thus understanding David's fancy flights
As in the Psalms he bares his straying soul.
But from the depths he looks to God, his goal,
And with that look is raised to glorious heights.
Ah, hope within the Psalms shall far transcend
The best that earthly poets may have penned.

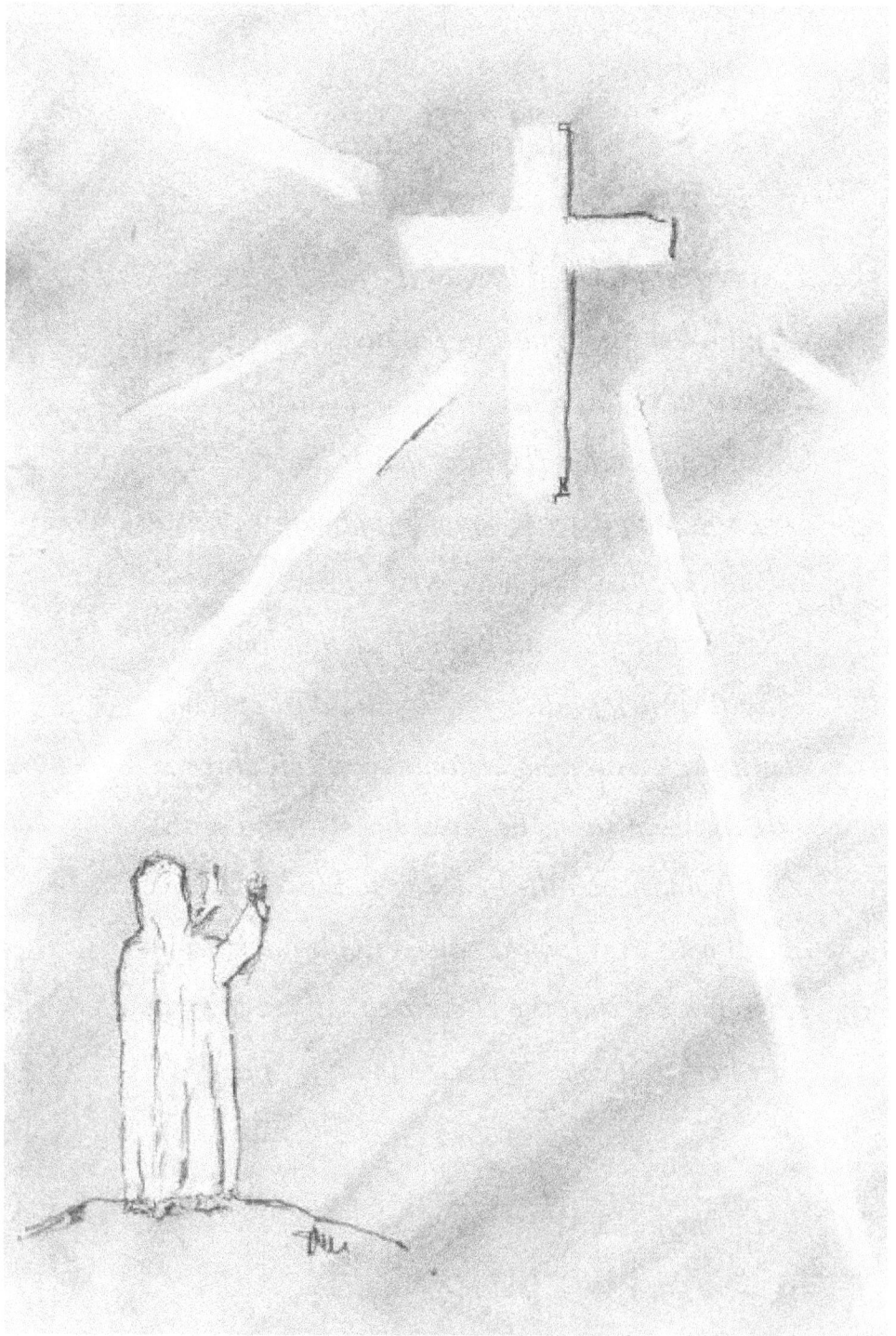

3

In The Sight Of God

The blinkered sight that's owned by mortal man
Sees but a part of what is in man's soul;
And man himself would not reveal the whole
Of thoughts and deeds; all parts of his life's span.
He, cunningly with chosen words, reveals
But portions of his character to show
To worldly gaze; there is no need to know
The sinful side he carefully conceals.
But God, the Lord of all creation, knows
Not only deeds and words, but thoughts as well;
And yet His Son has felt the pangs of hell,
To clothe with righteousness the ones He chose.
How can I help but give Him all due praise
Who loves me so, in spite of His pure gaze?

4

Peace And Love

Forget those things which do not foster love;
Ill feelings, or sad memories of hurts,
Like vengeful thoughts, or wishing just desserts
That puts another down in 'push and shove.'
How often will a needless hurt persist
Yet which so quickly could be put at rest
By either one not seeking their own best;
Love is not helped when selves for self insist.
Instead, absorb a critic's harsh remark,
Go gently then, and seek the peaceful way;
Humility, not pride, shall save the day;
The soft response may quench the angry spark.
Embrace that which shall give a peaceful plan,
Remember that great love God has for man.

5

Candles

See how each candle's fitful guttering glow
Spreads little light where once it brightly shone,
For now those burning wicks are almost gone;
And all too soon there'll be no flame to show
Where once they burned and spread their cheery rays.
For times are passed when they lit far and wide
And now it's only those who stand beside
Who see, concerned, each candle's closing phase.
How quickly is the span of life consumed,
How soon, it seems, the years of life are spent.
And some, for wasted years, would yet repent;
A candle's span should never be assumed.
And may my candle's flame, itself not bright,
Impart, from Christ Himself, God's greater light.

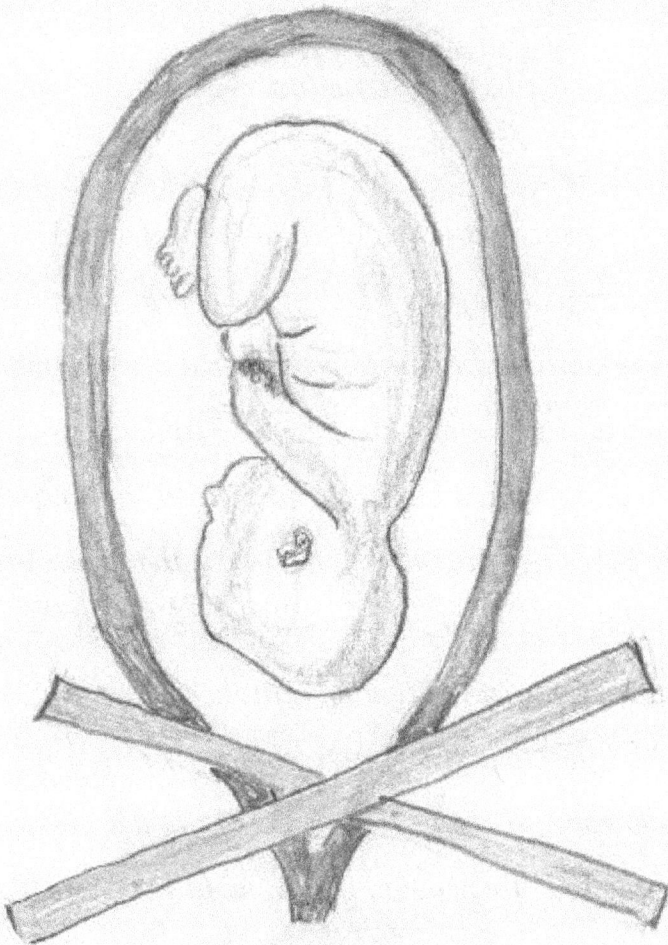

6

The Sanctity Of Life

Oh God, how far is man allowed to go
Before your sovereign hand shall call a halt?
When shall his cup be filled with evil fault,
And then its brim, with blood, shall overflow?
Infanticide? Abortion is the name
For such a course of self expedience.
A thrill without the inconvenience.
Society now seldom sees the shame.
To kill is an indictable offence.
Yet life, when still confined within the womb,
With conscience free, consign it to the tomb?
But life is life, so where's the moral sense?
Your holiness has long now been ignored,
But man has yet to answer to you, Lord.

7

No Grief For Me

No grief for me, or rather, not too great,
Since this tired tent, at last, has welcomed death,
And listless lungs are now devoid of breath;
For this is but the way of mankind's fate.
The soul that sins is surely set to die,
And I have been no better than the rest;
But through the death of Christ I now am blessed
For He, in love, once heard my humble cry.
And Christ has done what mankind cannot do;
No matter where the yesterdays I trod,
I have become the righteousness of God.
That promise made by loving grace is true.
And now I see my Saviour face to face;
Salvation, not of works, but all of grace!

8

Destruction And Mercy

The leaders call to courage in the face
Of earthquake, fire, and flood; but we have seen
The best of human power can't intervene
When such events have struck at frightening pace.
How powerless the great are proven then.
When buildings shake and mountains split apart,
Despair all round might break the bravest heart;
But God sits sovereign over earth and men.
And these disasters, large though they appear,
Are small compared to that which is to come.
God's outpoured wrath, for sin, is fearsome;
And well might man have reason then to fear.
God's wrath is great; His mercy more than great
For all who come to Christ, their advocate.

LIFE

BIRTH

DEATH

9

How Can A Man?

How can a man be sure to find his way
Through life's unknown and indistinctive maze,
With twists and turns and unknown future days?
Small wonder some have hearts filled with dismay.
But there are those who, with self-confidence,
Look straight ahead, turn neither left nor right,
Fulfil their own ambitions with delight;
Yet do not know their last line of defence.
For God requires that each shall give account;
But none has lived the life that should have been,
Our slate of life is not presented clean;
It's soiled by sin, even the least amount.
How then is man to live aright life's story?
Walk with the Lord, and He shall lead to glory.

JERUSALEM TIMES
VICTORY
MANY IN CORINTH REPENT AND TURN TO CHRIST.
DAILY FORUM
ROME
THE APOSTLE PAUL
CORINTHIAN NEWS LIMITED
CORINTH TURNED UPSIDE DOWN
AS THE APOSTLE PAUL. PREACHES TO MASIVE CROWDS.
GALILEE TIMES.
GOSPEL PREACHED IN CORINTH.
NEW CHURCH FOR THE CITY AS MANY REPENT AND FOLLOW CHRIST
PAUL SAYS

10

Corinthian Victory

The travellers, traders, merchants, and the sharks,
Together with the prostitutes and thieves
Cared nothing for behaviour which aggrieves;
Where selfish godless morals left their marks.
And this was Corinth under Roman rule;
The centre of a hedonistic trade
Where every opportunist had it made,
Where one who lived aright was thought a fool.
But God had called a man whom He had sought
To preach good news on that unholy ground;
And there were some God's Spirit turned around,
Who listened as the purer things were taught.
If God could claim a victory in that town,
Take courage, for He still can claim a crown.

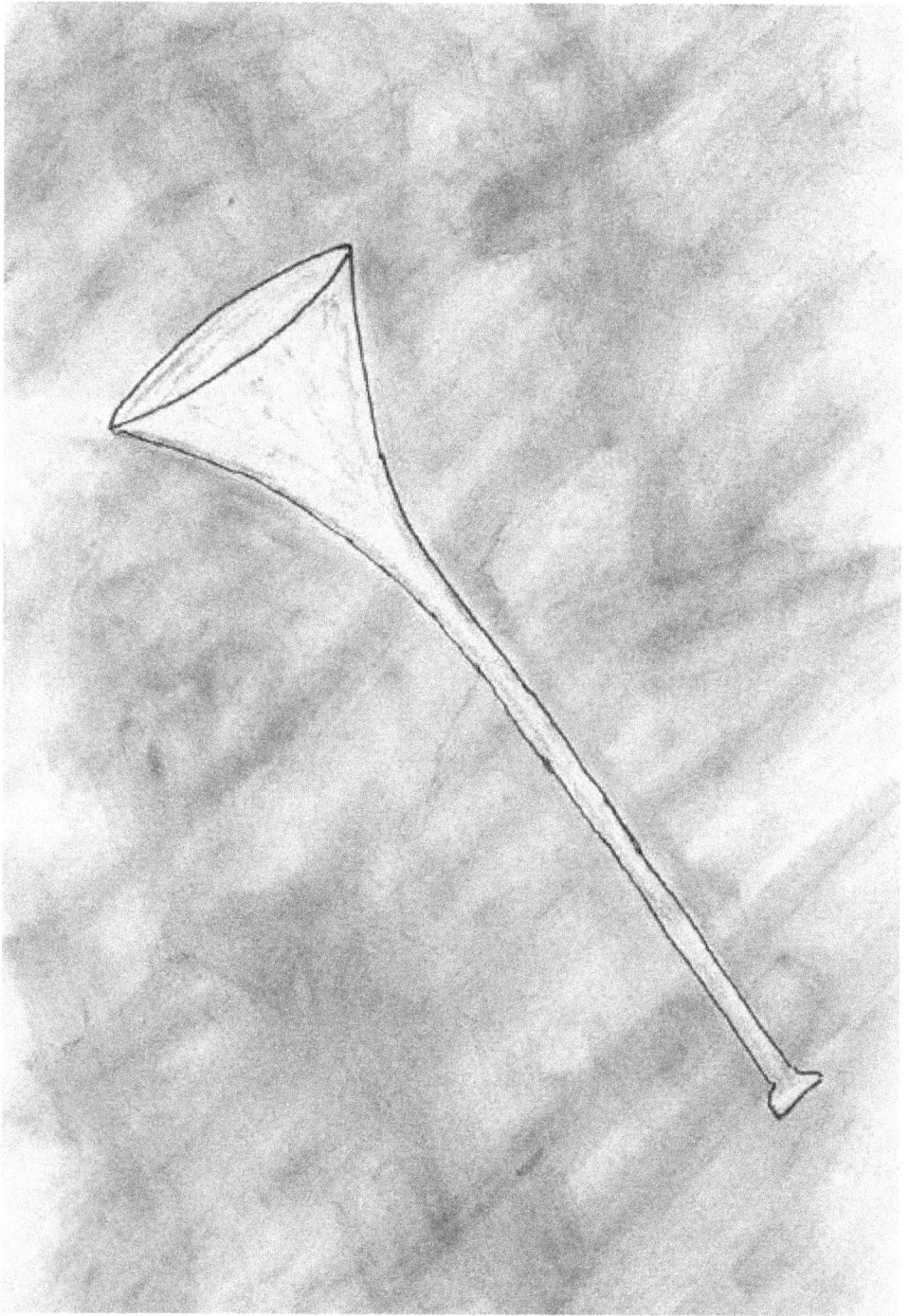

11

Ready For The Trumpet

Cacophonies of life, a constant clamour,
All fighting for a place in every soul;
They constantly will wheedle and cajole
To sell themselves with artificial glamour.
And creeds and cults declaim both long and loud,
To captivate allegiance for a vote,
While merchants cry out from a moneyed throat
Their products make you beautiful or proud.
But in amongst this clash of worldly din
Are smaller calls whose message is profound,
But too few heed this urgent warning sound;
They're deafened by the deadly work of sin.
Yet there'll be just those few who shall, at last,
Rejoice to hear God's trumpet's final blast.

12

The Doer of Great Things

Who is the man whose might can do great things?
Who is the one whose wit sets him apart
Above his fellows with his clever art,
And, sometimes proud, in self-expression, sings?
But not all have the province of great gifts;
For some are seen to be far less endowed;
Considered then as little in the crowd,
In whose direction praise so seldom shifts.
The high-born man could not choose gifts at birth,
Nor did the serf throw any gifts aside,
For God alone has, by His will, supplied
The skills and strength for every man on earth.
His might works through the foolish and the weak,
Confounding those who love to proudly speak.

13

Does Envy?

Does envy gnaw your heart when all around
Are players on the stage of life who seem
To live a life of which most only dream;
Where luxuries and pleasures both abound?
And many have no thought of others' pains.
The drug lord, and the con-man, and the thief,
The shady business man who causes grief,
Enjoy the fruits of their ill-gotten gains.
Their few brief years on earth shall soon pass by,
Then all the comforts they have ever known
Shall vanish as they reap what they have sown;
To opt for this world's wealth is Satan's lie.
There's nothing to be envied at their end
Who face God as a judge, and not a friend.

14

Roll Call

The news came through today of yet one more
Whose feet shall never tread this earth again.
A friend from years ago has done with pain,
And left behind him hearts now grieved and sore.
But, such is life, the way of man on earth,
Whose times and seasons are by God ordained,
Whose every breath is by that God sustained,
And every journey set, to death from birth.
And when my name is called to take my place,
At some time which no mortal man can know,
I shall not then rehearse my deeds to show
I have the right to meet God face to face.
For all my best is soiled with sin's taint;
But Christ has taken all of my complaint.

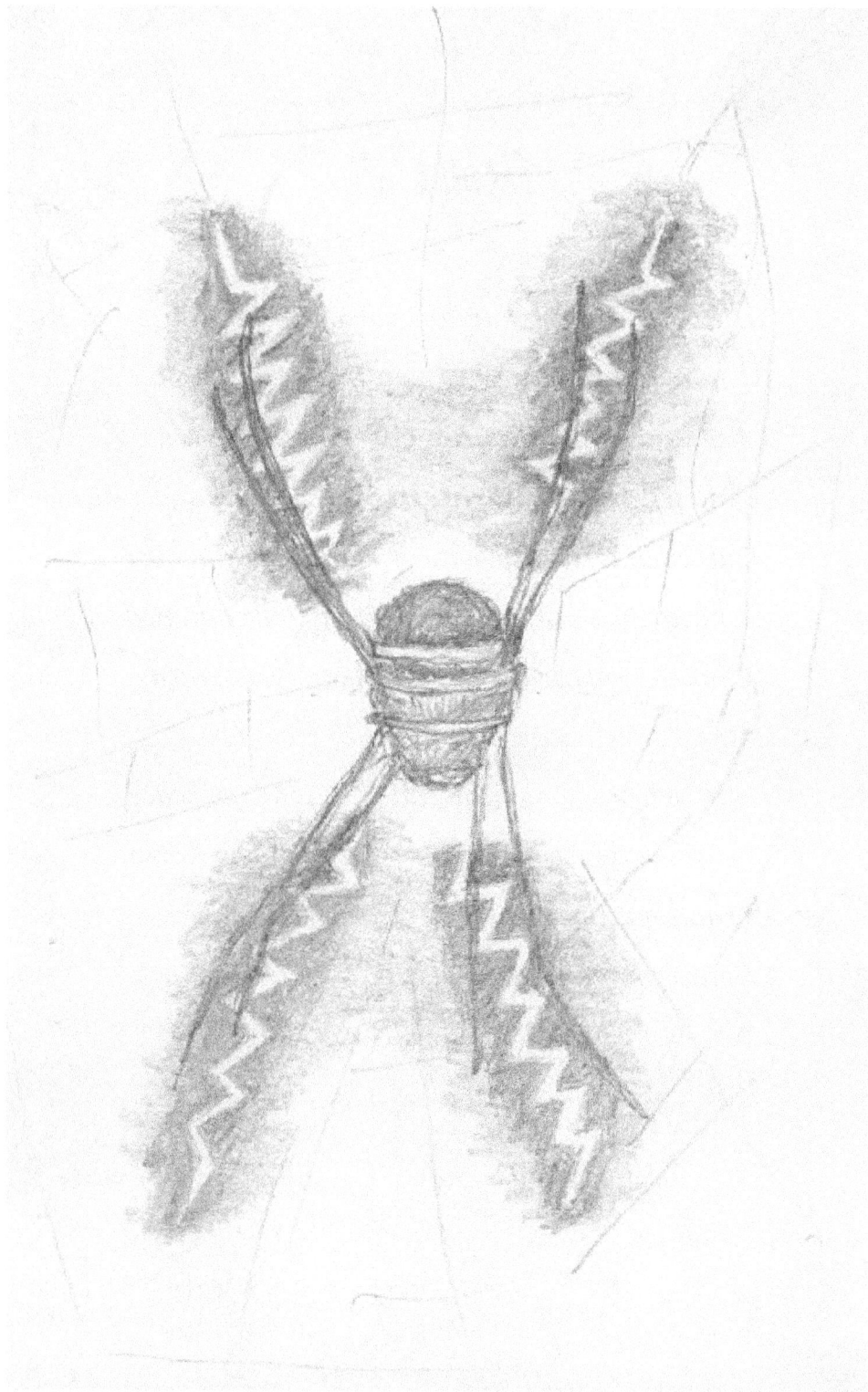

15

Not As A Spider

Not as a spider, casting threads afloat
To catch the whim of any passing breeze,
To anchor down wherever they may please;
So then to spin its fragile silken cote.
Not as a spider, with no certain plan,
Who rather seems to leave it all to fate,
Then passively and silently shall wait
For meal or mate, a mere arachnidan.
Not as a spider, but as one whose course
Is in the hand of God, the one true guide,
May man embark on his life's time and tide,
And come to journey's end without remorse.
And many spin a fragile silken thread;
But others trust that heavenly guide instead.

16

How Blind Are Those

How blind are those who cannot see the truth;
A veil is drawn across each darkened mind,
And wasted is the wealth of years combined
For old age now has long supplanted youth.
The sprinkled truth received across those years
Has all been swept aside in sad neglect.
And truth now says there's judgement to expect;
In ignorance the spirit has no fears.
But ignorance, so born, shall not withdraw
The truth of judgement for a sinful soul,
Whose heavenward search is but a forlorn goal;
But rather sin's reward for evermore.
There is a hope: cry from that veil's dark place,
None is refused who seeks the Saviour's face.

GOD SAID: "I AM WHO I AM" Exodus 3:14

"I THE LORD DO NOT CHANGE" Malachi 3:6

17

The Dilution of God

When men think less of God than what they ought
And cast Him as just slightly greater than
One of themselves, egalitarian,
One to be bargained with, or even bought;
They also then belittle His demands,
His majesty and power they put aside.
Then, with a sort of self delusional pride,
Their destiny, they think, is in their hands.
And words of disobedience are changed:
Adultery becomes just 'an affair',
And sin, a 'misdemeanour' here and there:
Opinions of those souls by sin deranged.
God's glory and His ways are absolute,
His majesty and power He'll not dilute.

The heavens declare the glory of God; the skies proclaim the work of his hands.

PSALM 19:1

18

The Glory of God

The Lord, our God speaks with such awesome power
That merely at His word the heavens were formed;
And stellar matter fiercely burned and stormed:
A show of might to make the bravest cower.
This Lord dwells in a high and holy place,
So far beyond the reach of sinful men,
And yet, is pleased to dwell with sinners when
They humbly, with contrition, live by grace.
For God created man to walk with Him.
But man, made in God's own similitude,
By his antagonistic attitude,
Destroyed communion by a thoughtless whim.
Magnificent is that salvation plan
That Deity should deign to come as man.

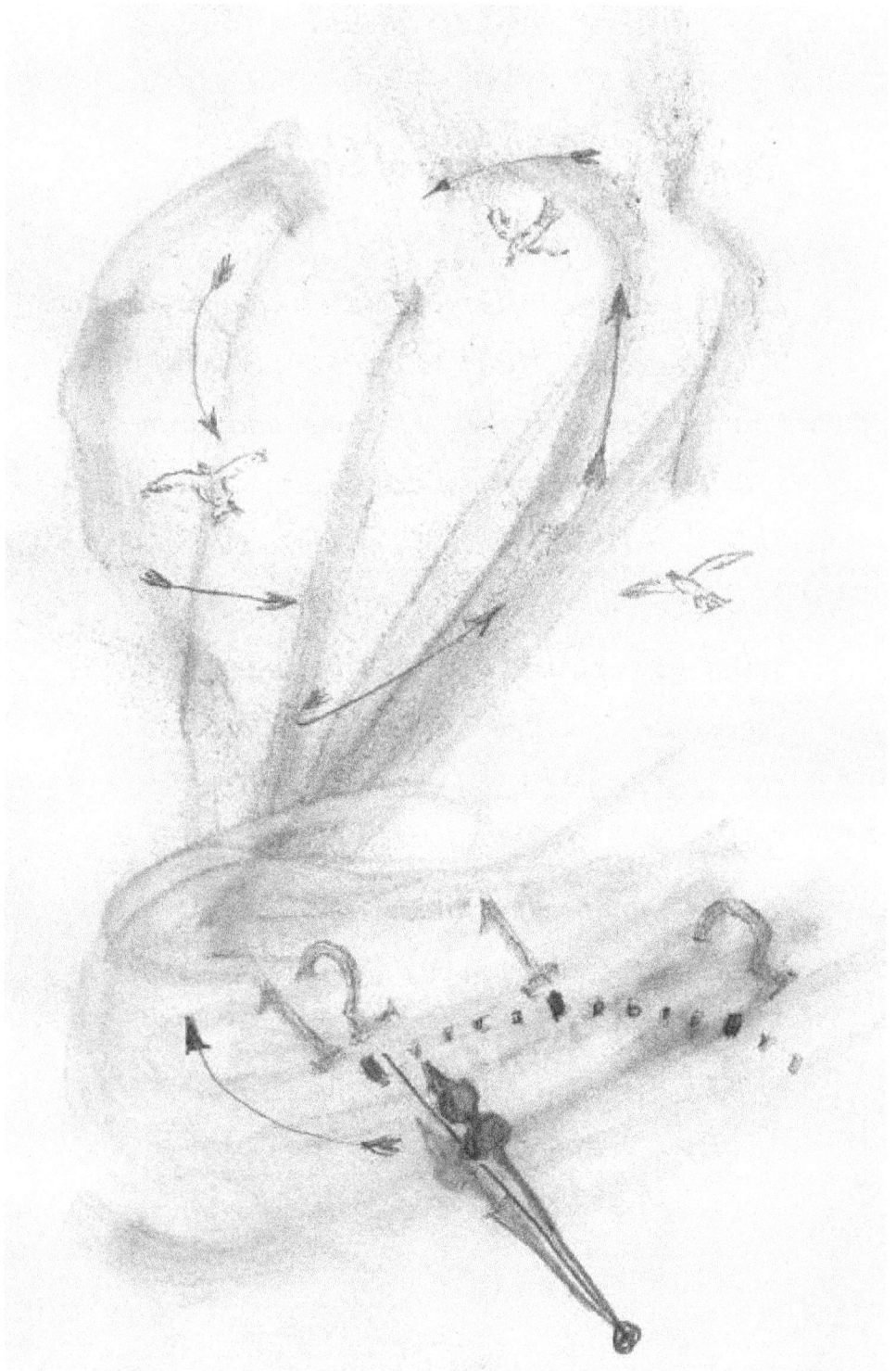

19

The Unguarded Word

Unguarded words uttered in careless haste,
Or harshly spat, with anger's venom filled;
The words that tell of hatred, hard and chilled,
Or gossip when the victim shan't be faced,
Reveal the speaker's soul, bereft of care.
And with harsh words seeds of ill will are sown,
For in those careless moments truth is shown:
True feelings of the speaker's heart laid bare.
And in that instant, words, like birds, have fled,
Like wind-blown dust, can never be called back;
Those arrows with their pointed cruel attack.
One wishes they might never have been said.
But when the heart has purer things interred
There is no need to fear th'unguarded word.

20

Focus

When God of old unleashed His awesome power
With plague and pestilence to show His hand,
To cause a drought throughout a kingdom's land,
Or rain hailstones at His appointed hour;
Such things took place according to His word
That His decree and purpose be fulfilled,
That knowledge, as He said, might be instilled:
"That all the nations know *I am the Lord.*"
But natural man will focus far below
The elevated worship God demands,
And wants that God should bow to his commands:
Such actions put man's ignorance on show.
God does not act for man's success and fame:
Ascribe to God the glory due His name.

21

Coming Glory

In vain so many chase the youthful dream,
In vain so many fight the cracking crust
Of this decaying product of the dust,
Which must conform to mankind's destined stream.
Still, many heed the subtle seller's call
To buy that which delays the signs of age;
But time shall win the war that he will wage
As every ploy shall ultimately fall.
But some will let this earthly glory fade;
They have a promise, be they king or slave,
Which leads to glory far beyond the grave,
And far beyond mere human accolade:
When Jesus Christ, who is their life, appears
They'll have a glory past the reach of years.

22

It's Sad To Hear

It's sad to hear that life is running out
For one whose day of grace is almost passed.
The die for his eternity seems cast:
No certainty, but forlorn hope and doubt.
A life of works is all that he can show;
His works were good, his deeds were kind, and yet
There's nothing there to bridge the gulf that's set
Between the Lord and sinful man below.
I plead that he might understand and know
That grace shall come from Jesus Christ alone;
There is no other way he might atone
For sin. His end is now so close, and, though
One fears the unrepentant sinner's plight,
Shall not the Judge of all the earth do right?

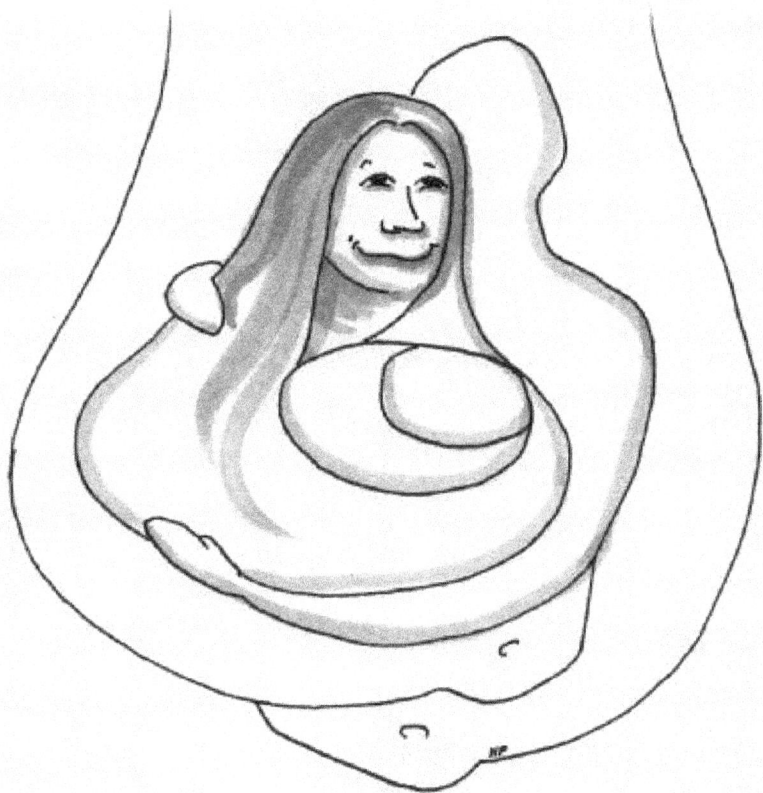

23

She Smiled

She smiled and held her new-born to her breast,
The miracle of childbirth was with her;
And twice again this image would recur.
She smiled, as through the years, she had been blest.
She smiled to see the graciousness of God,
As with her spouse they'd made Him their life's guide.
His strength for them was proven and was tried,
With comfort from God's promised staff and rod.
So looking back to see the life God planned,
She smiled again, a grateful, tired soul,
And thanked the Lord; but time had taken toll.
She weakly smiled and held her lover's hand.
The sheet was drawn in silence in that ward;
She smiled in death, for she had seen her Lord.

24

Grief

Sin is the root of all our human grief,
When life turns to a path we had not planned,
Events we neither want nor understand
Imposed with neither warning nor relief.
For many times we forego personal gain
When man-made plans have somehow gone astray,
We suffer loss when things are snatched away,
Relationships destroyed, we feel the pain.
If only men with God were still as one,
They'd understand that their lives' tracks were planned
As God has all of history in his hand.
But sin has brought that fellowship undone.
We shan't traverse this life without a tear
While waiting for our Saviour to appear.

25

Satisfaction

Consider the creation of the Lord,
How everything He made was very good;
And still His work is perfect, so we should
Be satisfied; with Him be in accord.
Unknowable to us are thoughts and ways
That God in His good pleasure has designed;
Inscrutable to any finite mind
That we should know this God beyond all praise.
But we, by sinful nature, are at war
With God, who has His own agenda set;
And when our aspirations are not met
His actions we so readily deplore.
Full satisfaction comes no other way
Than being in God's hand, soft yielding clay.

26

Defiled

These feet have followed many selfish ways
And walked away from paths which God required;
These eyes have looked on what the flesh desired
And turned far from an upward heavenly gaze.
This mind has dwelt on many sinful scenes
And often traced a secular pursuit;
And hands which quickly snatched forbidden fruit
Have often erred by various ways and means.
O God, your perfect image is defiled
By man's corrupted nature so ingrained.
How might eternal pardon be obtained?
And man to God again be reconciled?
The blood of Christ is all that could atone,
And He has purchased back what is His own.

27

Revelation

The vista of a frozen alpine peak
Where power has thrust it far towards the sky;
The things which can't be seen by human eye;
Design which makes each living thing unique;
The tidal wave which comes with dreaded swell;
The might with which an earthquake shakes the ground;
The fearsome storm which comes with thunderous sound
And lightning flash; all these have much to tell
Of sovereign God's creative power and might,
But nothing of His mercy and His grace
That's offered to a sinner in disgrace
Who will admit to his eternal plight.
These attributes of mercy, love, and grace
Are shown to those who've given Christ first place.

28

Lucinda*

Lucinda, you had lived before my time
But stories of your godliness were told
That even when you had grown weak and old
Your love for God still burned as in your prime.
I never knew the earnestness and care
With which you raised a family in your youth,
Where at your knee you taught each godly truth
To children who were gathered listening there.
Then in the last few fading twilight years,
The love of God you shared remained the same;
And pastors were encouraged when they came
To share with one for whom death held no fears.
A branch who grew in Christ, the vine and root,
Your life in old age still bore godly fruit.

* A great-grandmother of the author.

JOHN 1
14 And the Word became flesh
and dwelt among us and
we beheld his glory,
glory as of the Only Son
from the Father, full of
grace and truth.

29

Mysteries

The mysteries surrounding us each day
Yet exercise the human intellect,
So man will probe, and measure, and inspect.
The mystery of unknown things, (which may
Be solved if man's discovery is advanced)
Is limited to what he understands.
He can't surpass the reach of mind and hands,
Then only as his knowledge is enhanced.
But how did Jesus Christ become a man?
Both fully God and fully man in one?
Eternal Spirit; flesh and blood; His Son.
Inscrutable is God's salvation plan
Incomprehensible this mystery:
Eternal God stepped into history.

30

Why Did They Die?

O Lord, how much expression do we need
To have the evil heart of man revealed?
We see the broken lives which can't be healed;
Results of yet another evil deed.
The senseless slaughter of the innocents,
So many cut down cruelly in their prime,
The snuffing out of lives before their time,
For such a crime there is no recompense.
The blood of infants cries out from the ground,
Those tiny victims heartlessly destroyed
And snatched away from love they ere enjoyed.
Unhealable the grief now so profound.
This is unfettered evil in control;
God's grace alone can change man's darkened soul.

31

Strength

At times the spirit flags beneath the weight
Of burdens life imposes day by day,
And yet the creature often finds a way
To navigate each stress-imposing state.
But not all men can overcome the odds
Which seem at times so cruelly measured out,
And even life itself may seem in doubt
If man just looks at all his self-made gods.
For gods which man has made are wisps of thought
From searching darkened minds; they have no strength
To offer anything for life at length,
And cannot satisfy or give support.
But when man looks to God, by Whom he's made,
He'll find a real supporting power displayed.

IN THE NAME
of
THE FATHER & THE SON

&

THE HOLY SPIRIT

May God Bless You.

32

God Bless You

"And God bless you," the youthful voices said
As all the children greeted that day's guest;
An often quoted line one might suggest,
But was it from the heart, or just the head?
At such a tender age one often finds
There is no solid grasp of such a thought
In all its fullness; yet that truth was taught
To, possibly, repose in those young minds.
So therefore from that group there may be some
Who, as the years shall pass, shall recognise
That God in His great mercy, ever wise,
Does bless those who obey His call, and come.
I know such blessings from His hand are free;
In such amazing ways God blesses me.

33

For The Crimean Tatars

Pain, disbelief befalls each anxious friend
Responding to the saddening news that's heard.
Each, scarce believing every frightening word,
Can now but offer prayer that this shall end.
In times gone by these pogrom victims were
Oppressed and persecuted, some to death,
Unwanted as an ethnic shibboleth.
Satanic forces once again now stir.
The years have passed, but hearts of evil men
Are just as black as they have ever been,
Tyrannical, they work out sin's gangrene
And they have filled their cup of evil, when
Revenging God, who holds the hearts of kings,
Shall show His power and glory from these things.

"I AM THE LORD I DO NOT CHANGE"

34

Beyond The River (1)

If we could see beyond the final stream,
The inescapable dark stream of death;
(And death first came in judgement on man's breath);
Perhaps we'd see the fullness of God's scheme
Where judgement still must fall as justly right,
For God, and His pronouncements must remain.
The soul that sins is ordained to be slain;
The fate of all unrighteous in His sight.
"I am the Lord," He said, "I do not change."
But He would show His love to sinful man
With such a merciful salvation plan;
Our sin for righteousness by Christ exchange.
To cross that stream of death need hold no fear
For all who've come to Christ and hold Him dear.

Life   Death.

35

Beyond The River (2)

But there beyond that river's farthest shore
The gaping mouth of hell's awful abyss
Stands ready to receive all who dismiss
The mercy God extends to rich and poor.
For there is no divide by human scale
As all mankind falls infinitely short
Of God's perfection. Christ alone has bought
Release where man's best deeds can only fail.
It's God Himself who holds life's flimsy thread
Of all mankind; life ends when none can tell.
Then some shall go to glory, some to hell;
Some leave this earth with joy, and some with dread.
We do not know which day shall be our last,
Tomorrow might well be God's grace has passed.

... the righteousness that
comes from God
and is by faith.

philippians 3:9 niv

36

Beyond The River (3)

And when, at last, we cross this final stream,

This inescapable dark stream of death,

And these clay dwellings are devoid of breath,

No longer might we live an earthly dream,

For hoping and imagination then

Shall be replaced by truth so understood,

And all shall see that God alone is good

And is a being far above all men.

Shall not the Judge of all the earth do right?

His judgement shall be shown to be correct;

The slightest evil soul He must reject.

But mercy may put man's sin out of sight.

For all who saw for their sin, Jesus died,

God shall, through Christ, for them be satisfied.

But as it is written,

"what no eye has seen, nor ear heard, nor the heart of man imagined,

what God has prepared for those who love Him"

1 Corinthians 2:9

English Standard Version

37

Beyond The River (4)

And there awaits for each and every saint,
(For all who have embraced the grace of God
And crossed the stream of death unscathed, dry-shod,
Against whom God has now not one complaint),
A life beyond man's self-indulgent dreams.
For heaven is not what earthly man may think:
A peaceful life of pleasure, food, and, drink,
Surrounded by imaginative schemes.
For mortal man, with neither mind nor heart,
Can hope to know the things that are prepared
For those who love Him, so God has declared.
But by His Spirit shall such truth impart.
And times of quiet, spent with God alone,
Foreshadow times around His kingly throne.

'Forsaken by God ... It is finished.'

38

What Was The Pain?

When was the last time that you shed a tear
In humble thanks for that great sacrifice
Of Christ, who left eternal paradise
To live as mortal man, and suffer here?
The scourging with the flesh torn from the bone,
The crucifixion nails driven through
His hands and feet; and all of this He knew
Was not the worst He must endure alone.
For not a word was said of such great pain,
But, rather, that forsaken cry to God.
He bore, on that vicarious path He trod,
The wrath of God that sinful man might gain.
Eternal Godhead fellowship was torn
That man's ungodly soul might be reborn.

For the wisdom of this world is folly with GOD.

1 CORINTHIANS 3:19
ENGLISH STANDARD VERSION.

39

Godly Wisdom

How can the dead describe what truly lives?
Or else the living gain help from the dead?
Or stopped ears understand what has been said?
How can blind eyes see wonders that light gives?
Do we expect a corpse to rise in power?
Do we expect the ignorant to lead?
The uninformed to answer every need?
Yet all around it takes place every hour.
For many will, by human thinking, try
Explaining Godly wisdom from a mind
Which, without God, is spiritually blind,
And shed light on eternal things. They lie.
For only those to whom God gives His light
Can understand eternal things aright.

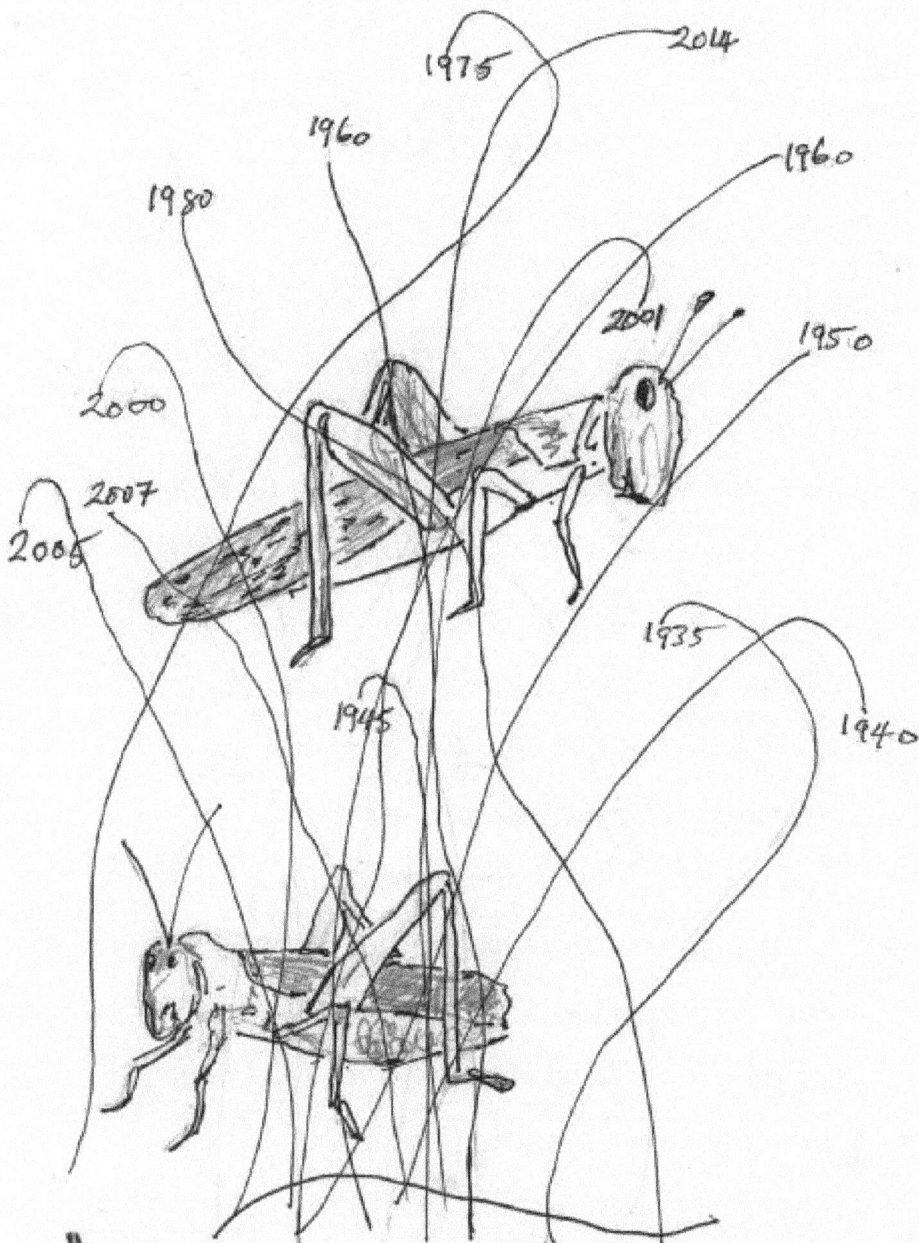

"I will restore the years that the locusts have eaten."

40

Restoration

Those years which seem both wasted and devoured,
The years when opportunities were lost,
When boundaries deliberately were crossed
And life became a burden, somewhat soured,
Have brought about a sighing and regret.
As locust plagues strip all before them bare,
So squandered years have nothing to declare,
And all seems just a hopeless loss, and yet
God hears the humble cry of those who turn
In penitence to Him; He will forgive,
Restoring flagging spirits so they live
And, being brought to life, perhaps to learn.
His mercy means His own are not forsaken;
He shall restore the years by locusts taken.

Peter said to Him "You shall
never wash my feet". Jesus
answered him "If I do not wash
you, you have no share with me".

Simon Peter said to Him "Lord
not my feet only but also my
hands and my head".
    John 13: 8-9 English Standard Version.

41

The Servant

Where is the man who has, throughout the years,
Discovered life's fulfilment in the sure
And certain path, unknown to him before,
But known to God, who can allay all fears?
Where is the man who has not flinched from fight,
But stood and faced the fierce foe of the soul,
And with the call of God held as his goal
Has kept the promises of God in sight?
That man stands tall amid the world's decay,
His weakness demonstrates a godly strength,
His foolishness, God's wisdom shown at length;
The power and work of God thus on display.
That man now stands, a testament to grace;
And sovereign will alone has set his place.

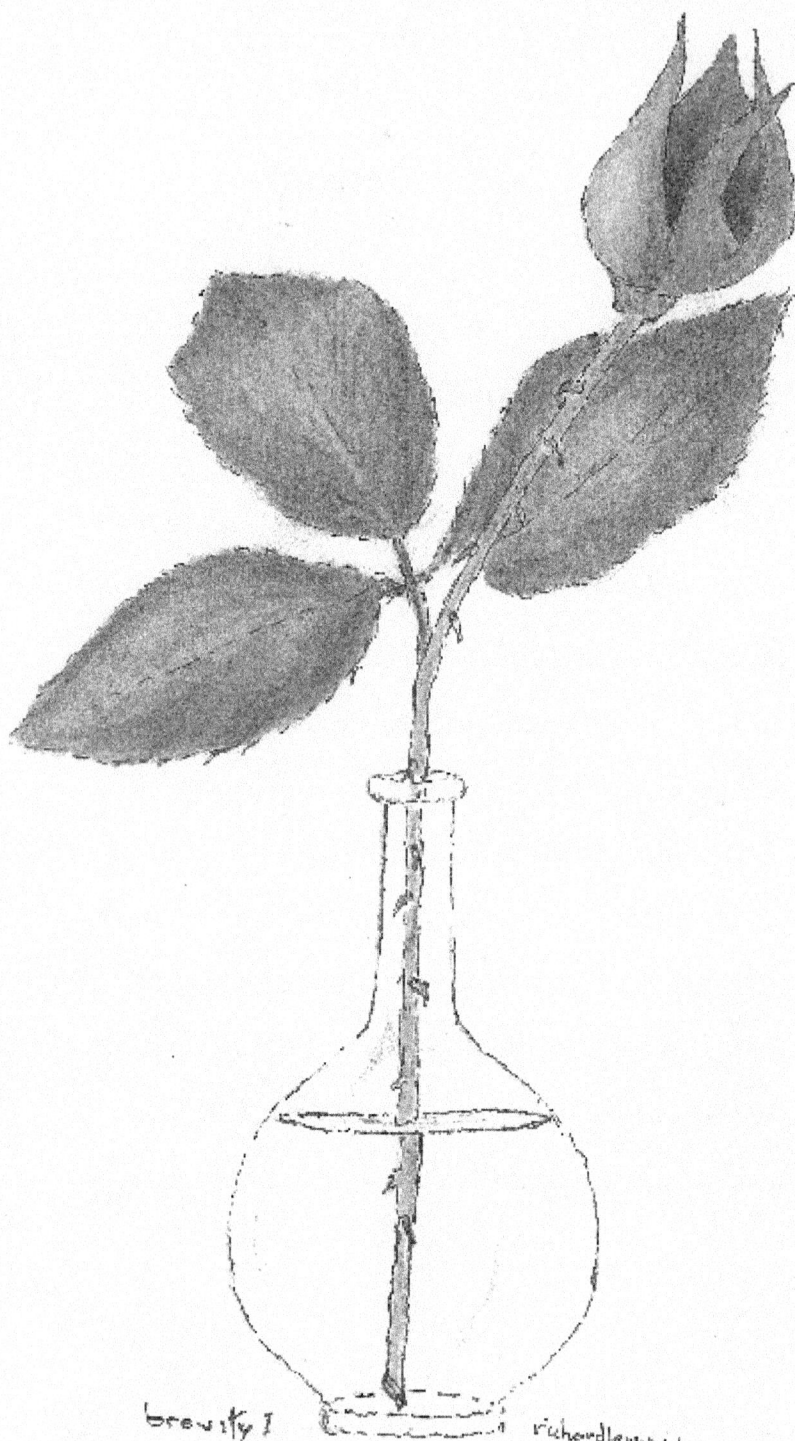

brevity 1   richardlewis 10/04

42

Brevity (1)

How fleeting are the years which span our time,
A few short wisps of quickly taken breath
Are all too soon consumed, engulfed by death,
And some are gone ere having reached their prime.
One cannot know the final curtain call
When plans and pleasures come to no account,
When effort and ambitions all amount
To nought for those who for themselves gave all.
Where such myopic views of life exist
And "carpe diem" is the daily cry,
Where ignorance hides truth which passes by,
Eternal life beyond this earth is missed.
Man is not made to live and fade away,
But dwell with God in perfect sinless day.

brevity 11   richardhawks 10/14

43

Brevity (2)

To dwell with God in perfect sinless day
Is where the soul of man is most at rest;
But many souls shall fail the final test.
Some from the gift of Christ have turned away,
Or some perhaps attracted by the thought
Of striving to achieve some personal goal,
Give little time to think about their soul;
Eternal needs are far from being sought.
For all of this world's castles and the fame
Or satisfaction that man searches for
Shall all too soon be gone to be no more,
And what then of pursuits and lifelong aim?
The lust of flesh, of eyes, and pride of life
Do not prepare to leave this world of strife.

breurty III   richardlewis 10/14

44

Brevity (3)

Do not prepare to leave this world of strife
With only deeds both kind and good to man;
For even though one does the best one can
It falls short of the mark. This world is rife
With those who would put forward their own case
Of how they've earned a home with God in heaven,
And argue that they're sure they should be given
An everlasting personal resting place.
Alas, the purity of God demands
A perfect life of total righteousness.
No man can claim a life of sinlessness,
So finds himself in God's avenging hands
For He is just; but mercy too is part
Of God's domain and His forgiving heart.

brevity 14   richard lewis 10/14.

45

Brevity (4)

Of God's domain and His forgiving heart
Is mercy granted, though it's not for all,
But is reserved for only those who call
On Christ, admitting that they had no part
In their salvation. His great sacrifice
Has paid in full the price that God requires
To save a soul from hell's eternal fires:
His death and resurrection shall suffice.
But many yet still do not see this boon;
And many seem to be afraid to tell
A dying world that all is far from well.
And opportunity shall pass too soon.
Days seem too few to spread this truth sublime;
How fleeting are the years which span our time!

46

Consider

Consider the immensity of space,
The canopy above beset with light
With sun by day, then sparkling jewels by night;
And with His word God holds it all in place.
Consider all God's care for His creation;
The air we breathe, the strength for every day;
His mercy far and wide thus on display;
For all are blessed without discrimination.
But greater than His mercy is His grace
He showers on all those He calls His own,
Who from eternity are named and known,
For whom Christ died, and took their sins' disgrace.
His universal mercy shall not last,
His grace goes on when time and space have passed.

H.P.

Some think that the journey should take precedence, as of the destination doesn't count; take in the events of life, which we absorb, its varied sights. And why not? For this world is full of the only way, some think, to the new and only way, never-ending beauties. Explore few, for this world is full of a a new, and though the events of life, no matter what we've seen of all the sights and sounds few, for this world is full of a such a destination doesn't and though the journey's choice may be of all the sights and seen moments only as if the journey never-ending and never-ending... there is a time to keep thoughts and moments, and suddenly, as if the destination doesn't a place in heaven to keep sounds of the world in sight, the Son of God, he is only way, some think that the treasure one can ill afford own in new sight but now, suddenly, as if the destination doesn't journey though, is not worthy take place on earth, the Son of God, he is only way, some think that the the path is set, man should own in new sight but how far have such a journey's choice may the journey should think take in events by experience. There have we go lose such a destination doesn't count; take in events by experience. For this world a where to keep the journey never-ending absorb its varied sights but now, suddenly, as if the destination doesn't journey's choice.

And why not? For this sights in sight, the Son of God, he is only way, some to explore, there is yet more to the world and though the journey never-ending... again, there is yet more to the world and though he is only way, some think that the of all the sights and sounds if the Son of God, he is only way, some think that the There is a place to keep in heaven, around and never-ending journey. Sight, a place in heaven to keep the only destination doesn't count; take in is its own reward, where the goal, now and never-ending journey should count; take in to lose such a treasure one the only destination doesn't count; take in on right. The path is set, man should own in sight, around and never-ending journey should count; take in have I say: The Son of God, he is only way, some think that the destination doesn't count; take in he is only way, some think that the destination doesn't count; take in precedence, as of the destination doesn't count; take in

47

Travelling

Some think the journey should take precedence,
As if the destination doesn't count;
Take in events of life, which quickly mount,
Absorb its varied sights and incidents.
And why not? For this world is full of new
And never-ending beauties to explore,
No matter what we've seen, there is yet more;
Of all the sights and sounds, we know but few.
There is a time to keep the goal in sight;
A place in heaven is its own reward,
To lose such treasure one can ill afford;
This journey, though, is not our choice of right.
The path is set for every mortal's day;
The Son of God—He is the only way.

H.P.

48

Rest (1)

No one is free from trials which life brings,
Those trials which are common to mankind,
By which the course of life is most defined.
The harshly-spoken word so quickly stings,
Obstructions too may thwart our plans and schemes
The ways we most desired have not worked out,
And confidence is gone; replaced with doubt,
Then all we seem to have are shattered dreams.
But is this all from life we may expect?
Is there no more than striving constantly
With each and every unknown vagary
Of life? We sometimes wonder and reflect.
But faith in God can calm the path of man
That God decreed before the world began.

49

Rest (2)

God has decreed, before the world began,
With wisdom which we cannot understand,
The course of hist'ry, which His sovereign hand
Must bring to pass, as there is but one plan.
For He is sovereign, and against Him none
Can bring a scheme, and hope by such to thwart
God's set decree; and so against Him nought
Can stand, for always shall His will be done.
But mankind does not have that wider view
From where God's fixed eternal plans were made;
A blinkered scene is what man sees displayed;
Small wonder man may think there's no way through.
But Jesus says, to mankind so distressed:
"Come all to me, and I will give you rest".

50

Rest (3)

"Come all to me and I will give you rest";
Such sure and certain words from Christ the Lord,
And words that all mankind can ill afford
To cast aside, by which they may be blest.
These words of truth came from the lips of one
Who only spoke the truth; from one who said,
"I'll rise again," and came back from the dead,
Thus proof enough, the power of God's Son.
And from the Christ of all omnipotence
Comes such an invitation to receive
A rest from Him for all who would believe;
To rest with one who knows and cares makes sense
Of what our life and death are all about,
And burdens one may carry with some doubt.

51

Rest (4)

The burdens one may carry with some doubt
That what one understands may be unsure,
That beyond what one knows, there may be more
Which plays a part in how each life turns out.
Who can foresee the unexpected turn?
Or what disasters may yet lie ahead?
There is no crystal ball which may be read,
No glimpse into the future one may earn.
But certainty is offered for all those
Who place their trust in Jesus, sovereign Lord,
Whose perfect love is infinitely broad.
The child of God rests in His care, and knows
It's one of those inconsequential things
That none is free from trials which life brings.

52

Rejoice

What if the day be difficult and long?
What if the spirit flags beneath the load?
And when the journey's on an unknown road
Where does one turn among the trampling throng?
So in the world, when turmoil seems to reign,
Where plans, both small and great, go unfulfilled,
And life itself runs counter to what's willed,
Where best of human effort seem in vain
Rejoice! It's Jesus Christ who sits supreme
Above the storms and tragedies and strife,
And sets the limits of each turn of life;
For he is Lord above each human scheme.
But greater is the joy, when, lastly blest,
The child of God shall know eternal rest.

Appendix 1

Associated Bible references

The Bible references given here are by no means exhaustive, but are a guide to the many thoughts and principles to be found in these sonnets. Most times it is advised to read around the suggested Bible passages to provide the context in which they appear.

1 "Harvest Time":   Psalms 39: 4-5
          1 Corinthians 15: 55-57

2 "The Psalms"   Psalms 119:97-99

3 "In The Sight Of God" Psalms 29: 1-2
          Jeremiah 17:9-10
          Ephesians 4: 23-24

4 "Peace And Love"   Micah 6:8
          Galatians 5:22-26

5 "Candles"   1 Chronicles 29:15
          Psalms 39:5
          Matthew 5:16
          Ephesians 2:10

23 "She Smiled" (cont'd)   Proverbs 3:6
                                   2 Corinthians 12:9

24 "Grief"   Genesis 3:17-19
                                   Job 23:10
                                   James 4:13-15

25 "Satisfaction"   Genesis 1
                                   Nehemiah 9:5
                                   Psalms 65:4
                                   Proverbs 19:23
                                   Isaiah 55:8
                                   Matthew 5:6

26 "Defiled"   Jeremiah 17:9
                                   Romans 5:9
                                   Ephesians 1:7
                                   Colossians 1:20
                                   1 John 1:7

27 "Revelation"   Romans 3:24
                                   Ephesians 1:7
                                   Ephesians 2:7-8
                                   Ephesians 6:24
                                   Colossians 1:17
                                   1 Timothy 1:14-16

41 "The Servant"
Matthew 25:14-23
1 Corinthians 1:27
2 Corinthians 12:10
Ephesians 2:10
Philippians 4:13

42 "Brevity (1)"
Psalms 39:4-7
Luke 12:16-21
James 4:14

43 "Brevity (2)"
Psalms 90:14
John 14:8
1 John 2:16

44 "Brevity (3)"
Ephesians 2:1-10

45 "Brevity (4)"
John 5:10
John 6:37
Acts 4:12
Ephesians 5:15-17
Colossians 4:5-6

46 "Consider"
Psalms 33:6
Isaiah 51:6
Matthew 5:45
2 Corinthians 6:2

47 "Travelling"

Psalms 73:24
Psalms 139:16
Matthew 16:26
John 12:25

48 "Rest (1)"

Job 5:7
Job 14:1
Matthew 11:28-30

49 "Rest (2)"

Psalms 147:12-18
Proverbs 19:21
Proverbs 21:1
Acts 17:26

50 "Rest (3)"

John 14:6
Ephesians 1:19-20
1 Peter 5:7

51 "Rest (4)"

Job 23:10
Psalms 73:23-24
Proverbs 3:5-6
James 4:13-17

52 "Rejoice"

Psalms 23:10
Ephesians 1:3
1 Thessalonians 5:18.

Appendix 2

Illustrations

Richard Lewis:

Nos. 1, 2, 3, 4, 5, 6, 7, 8, 9, 10, 11, 12, 13, 14, 15, 16, 17, 18, 19, 20, 21, 22, 24, 25, 26, 27, 29, 30, 31, 32, 34, 35, 36, 37, 38, 39, 40, 41, 42, 43, 44, 45

Heather Paterson:

Nos. 23, 33, 46, 47, 48, 49, 50, 51, 52

Family Photograph:

No. 28

www.ingramcontent.com/pod-product-compliance
Lightning Source LLC
Chambersburg PA
CBHW051721040426
42447CB00023B/518